THE GOAL OF SOCIALISM

E.J. RAEB

ISBN 13: 9781720266082

Blank Page

Is Communism
Is Higher Taxes
Is To Abolish Capitalism

Is Communism
Is Higher Taxes
Is To Abolish Capitalism

Is Communism
Is Higher Taxes
Is To Abolish Capitalism

Is Communism
Is Higher Taxes
Is To Abolish Capitalism

Is Communism
Is Higher Taxes
Is To Abolish Capitalism

Is Communism
Is Higher Taxes
Is To Abolish Capitalism

Is Communism
Is Higher Taxes
Is To Abolish Capitalism

Is Communism
Is Higher Taxes
Is To Abolish Capitalism

Is Communism
Is Higher Taxes
Is To Abolish Capitalism

Is Communism
Is Higher Taxes
Is To Abolish Capitalism

Is Communism
Is Higher Taxes
Is To Abolish Capitalism

Is Communism
Is Higher Taxes
Is To Abolish Capitalism

Is Communism
Is Higher Taxes
Is To Abolish Capitalism

Is Communism
Is Higher Taxes
Is To Abolish Capitalism

Is Communism
Is Higher Taxes
Is To Abolish Capitalism

Is Communism
Is Higher Taxes
Is To Abolish Capitalism

Is Communism
Is Higher Taxes
Is To Abolish Capitalism

Is Communism
Is Higher Taxes
Is To Abolish Capitalism

Is Communism
Is Higher Taxes
Is To Abolish Capitalism

Is Communism
Is Higher Taxes
Is To Abolish Capitalism

Is Communism
Is Higher Taxes
Is To Abolish Capitalism

Is Communism
Is Higher Taxes
Is To Abolish Capitalism

Is Communism
Is Higher Taxes
Is To Abolish Capitalism

Is Communism
Is Higher Taxes
Is To Abolish Capitalism

Is Communism
Is Higher Taxes
Is To Abolish Capitalism

Is Communism
Is Higher Taxes
Is To Abolish Capitalism

Is Communism
Is Higher Taxes
Is To Abolish Capitalism

Is Communism
Is Higher Taxes
Is To Abolish Capitalism

Is Communism
Is Higher Taxes
Is To Abolish Capitalism

Is Communism
Is Higher Taxes
Is To Abolish Capitalism

Is Communism
Is Higher Taxes
Is To Abolish Capitalism

Is Communism
Is Higher Taxes
Is To Abolish Capitalism

Is Communism
Is Higher Taxes
Is To Abolish Capitalism

Is Communism
Is Higher Taxes
Is To Abolish Capitalism

Is Communism
Is Higher Taxes
Is To Abolish Capitalism

Is Communism
Is Higher Taxes
Is To Abolish Capitalism

Is Communism
Is Higher Taxes
Is To Abolish Capitalism

Is Communism
Is Higher Taxes
Is To Abolish Capitalism

Is Communism
Is Higher Taxes
Is To Abolish Capitalism

Is Communism
Is Higher Taxes
Is To Abolish Capitalism

Is Communism
Is Higher Taxes
Is To Abolish Capitalism

Is Communism
Is Higher Taxes
Is To Abolish Capitalism

Is Communism
Is Higher Taxes
Is To Abolish Capitalism

Is Communism
Is Higher Taxes
Is To Abolish Capitalism

Is Communism
Is Higher Taxes
Is To Abolish Capitalism

Is Communism
Is Higher Taxes
Is To Abolish Capitalism

Is Communism
Is Higher Taxes
Is To Abolish Capitalism

Is Communism
Is Higher Taxes
Is To Abolish Capitalism

Is Communism
Is Higher Taxes
Is To Abolish Capitalism

Is Communism
Is Higher Taxes
Is To Abolish Capitalism

Is Communism
Is Higher Taxes
Is To Abolish Capitalism

Is Communism
Is Higher Taxes
Is To Abolish Capitalism

Is Communism
Is Higher Taxes
Is To Abolish Capitalism

Is Communism
Is Higher Taxes
Is To Abolish Capitalism

Is Communism
Is Higher Taxes
Is To Abolish Capitalism

Is Communism
Is Higher Taxes
Is To Abolish Capitalism

Is Communism
Is Higher Taxes
Is To Abolish Capitalism

Is Communism
Is Higher Taxes
Is To Abolish Capitalism

Is Communism
Is Higher Taxes
Is To Abolish Capitalism

Is Communism
Is Higher Taxes
Is To Abolish Capitalism

Is Communism
Is Higher Taxes
Is To Abolish Capitalism

Is Communism
Is Higher Taxes
Is To Abolish Capitalism

Is Communism
Is Higher Taxes
Is To Abolish Capitalism

Is Communism
Is Higher Taxes
Is To Abolish Capitalism

Is Communism
Is Higher Taxes
Is To Abolish Capitalism

Is Communism
Is Higher Taxes
Is To Abolish Capitalism

Is Communism
Is Higher Taxes
Is To Abolish Capitalism

Is Communism
Is Higher Taxes
Is To Abolish Capitalism

Is Communism
Is Higher Taxes
Is To Abolish Capitalism

Is Communism
Is Higher Taxes
Is To Abolish Capitalism

Is Communism
Is Higher Taxes
Is To Abolish Capitalism

Is Communism
Is Higher Taxes
Is To Abolish Capitalism

Is Communism
Is Higher Taxes
Is To Abolish Capitalism

Is Communism
Is Higher Taxes
Is To Abolish Capitalism

Is Communism
Is Higher Taxes
Is To Abolish Capitalism

Is Communism
Is Higher Taxes
Is To Abolish Capitalism

Is Communism
Is Higher Taxes
Is To Abolish Capitalism

Is Communism
Is Higher Taxes
Is To Abolish Capitalism

Is Communism
Is Higher Taxes
Is To Abolish Capitalism

Is Communism
Is Higher Taxes
Is To Abolish Capitalism

Is Communism
Is Higher Taxes
Is To Abolish Capitalism

Is Communism
Is Higher Taxes
Is To Abolish Capitalism

Is Communism
Is Higher Taxes
Is To Abolish Capitalism

Is Communism
Is Higher Taxes
Is To Abolish Capitalism

Is Communism
Is Higher Taxes
Is To Abolish Capitalism

Is Communism
Is Higher Taxes
Is To Abolish Capitalism

Is Communism
Is Higher Taxes
Is To Abolish Capitalism

Is Communism
Is Higher Taxes
Is To Abolish Capitalism

Is Communism
Is Higher Taxes
Is To Abolish Capitalism

Is Communism
Is Higher Taxes
Is To Abolish Capitalism

Is Communism
Is Higher Taxes
Is To Abolish Capitalism

Is Communism
Is Higher Taxes
Is To Abolish Capitalism

Is Communism
Is Higher Taxes
Is To Abolish Capitalism

Is Communism
Is Higher Taxes
Is To Abolish Capitalism

Is Communism
Is Higher Taxes
Is To Abolish Capitalism

Is Communism
Is Higher Taxes
Is To Abolish Capitalism

Is Communism
Is Higher Taxes
Is To Abolish Capitalism

Is Communism
Is Higher Taxes
Is To Abolish Capitalism

Is Communism
Is Higher Taxes
Is To Abolish Capitalism

Is Communism
Is Higher Taxes
Is To Abolish Capitalism

Is Communism
Is Higher Taxes
Is To Abolish Capitalism

Is Communism
Is Higher Taxes
Is To Abolish Capitalism

Is Communism
Is Higher Taxes
Is To Abolish Capitalism

Is Communism
Is Higher Taxes
Is To Abolish Capitalism

Is Communism
Is Higher Taxes
Is To Abolish Capitalism

Is Communism
Is Higher Taxes
Is To Abolish Capitalism

Is Communism
Is Higher Taxes
Is To Abolish Capitalism

Is Communism
Is Higher Taxes
Is To Abolish Capitalism

Is Communism
Is Higher Taxes
Is To Abolish Capitalism

Is Communism
Is Higher Taxes
Is To Abolish Capitalism

Is Communism
Is Higher Taxes
Is To Abolish Capitalism

Is Communism
Is Higher Taxes
Is To Abolish Capitalism

Is Communism
Is Higher Taxes
Is To Abolish Capitalism

Is Communism
Is Higher Taxes
Is To Abolish Capitalism

Is Communism
Is Higher Taxes
Is To Abolish Capitalism

Is Communism
Is Higher Taxes
Is To Abolish Capitalism

Is Communism
Is Higher Taxes
Is To Abolish Capitalism

Is Communism
Is Higher Taxes
Is To Abolish Capitalism

Is Communism
Is Higher Taxes
Is To Abolish Capitalism

Is Communism
Is Higher Taxes
Is To Abolish Capitalism

Is Communism
Is Higher Taxes
Is To Abolish Capitalism

Is Communism
Is Higher Taxes
Is To Abolish Capitalism

Is Communism
Is Higher Taxes
Is To Abolish Capitalism

Is Communism
Is Higher Taxes
Is To Abolish Capitalism

Is Communism
Is Higher Taxes
Is To Abolish Capitalism

Is Communism
Is Higher Taxes
Is To Abolish Capitalism

Is Communism
Is Higher Taxes
Is To Abolish Capitalism

Is Communism
Is Higher Taxes
Is To Abolish Capitalism

Is Communism
Is Higher Taxes
Is To Abolish Capitalism

Is Communism
Is Higher Taxes
Is To Abolish Capitalism

Is Communism
Is Higher Taxes
Is To Abolish Capitalism

Is Communism
Is Higher Taxes
Is To Abolish Capitalism

Is Communism
Is Higher Taxes
Is To Abolish Capitalism

Is Communism
Is Higher Taxes
Is To Abolish Capitalism

Is Communism
Is Higher Taxes
Is To Abolish Capitalism

Is Communism
Is Higher Taxes
Is To Abolish Capitalism

Is Communism
Is Higher Taxes
Is To Abolish Capitalism

Is Communism
Is Higher Taxes
Is To Abolish Capitalism

Is Communism
Is Higher Taxes
Is To Abolish Capitalism

Is Communism
Is Higher Taxes
Is To Abolish Capitalism

Is Communism
Is Higher Taxes
Is To Abolish Capitalism

Is Communism
Is Higher Taxes
Is To Abolish Capitalism

Is Communism
Is Higher Taxes
Is To Abolish Capitalism

Is Communism
Is Higher Taxes
Is To Abolish Capitalism

Is Communism
Is Higher Taxes
Is To Abolish Capitalism

Is Communism
Is Higher Taxes
Is To Abolish Capitalism

Is Communism
Is Higher Taxes
Is To Abolish Capitalism

Is Communism
Is Higher Taxes
Is To Abolish Capitalism

Is Communism
Is Higher Taxes
Is To Abolish Capitalism

Is Communism
Is Higher Taxes
Is To Abolish Capitalism

Is Communism
Is Higher Taxes
Is To Abolish Capitalism

Is Communism
Is Higher Taxes
Is To Abolish Capitalism

Is Communism
Is Higher Taxes
Is To Abolish Capitalism

Is Communism
Is Higher Taxes
Is To Abolish Capitalism

Is Communism
Is Higher Taxes
Is To Abolish Capitalism

Is Communism
Is Higher Taxes
Is To Abolish Capitalism

Is Communism
Is Higher Taxes
Is To Abolish Capitalism

Is Communism
Is Higher Taxes
Is To Abolish Capitalism

Is Communism
Is Higher Taxes
Is To Abolish Capitalism

Is Communism
Is Higher Taxes
Is To Abolish Capitalism

Is Communism
Is Higher Taxes
Is To Abolish Capitalism

Is Communism
Is Higher Taxes
Is To Abolish Capitalism

Is Communism
Is Higher Taxes
Is To Abolish Capitalism

Is Communism
Is Higher Taxes
Is To Abolish Capitalism

Is Communism
Is Higher Taxes
Is To Abolish Capitalism

Is Communism
Is Higher Taxes
Is To Abolish Capitalism

Is Communism
Is Higher Taxes
Is To Abolish Capitalism

Is Communism
Is Higher Taxes
Is To Abolish Capitalism

Is Communism
Is Higher Taxes
Is To Abolish Capitalism

Is Communism
Is Higher Taxes
Is To Abolish Capitalism

Is Communism
Is Higher Taxes
Is To Abolish Capitalism

Is Communism
Is Higher Taxes
Is To Abolish Capitalism

Is Communism
Is Higher Taxes
Is To Abolish Capitalism

Is Communism
Is Higher Taxes
Is To Abolish Capitalism

Is Communism
Is Higher Taxes
Is To Abolish Capitalism

Is Communism
Is Higher Taxes
Is To Abolish Capitalism

Is Communism
Is Higher Taxes
Is To Abolish Capitalism

Is Communism
Is Higher Taxes
Is To Abolish Capitalism

Is Communism
Is Higher Taxes
Is To Abolish Capitalism

Is Communism
Is Higher Taxes
Is To Abolish Capitalism

Is Communism
Is Higher Taxes
Is To Abolish Capitalism

Is Communism
Is Higher Taxes
Is To Abolish Capitalism

Is Communism
Is Higher Taxes
Is To Abolish Capitalism

Is Communism
Is Higher Taxes
Is To Abolish Capitalism

Is Communism
Is Higher Taxes
Is To Abolish Capitalism

Is Communism
Is Higher Taxes
Is To Abolish Capitalism

Is Communism
Is Higher Taxes
Is To Abolish Capitalism

Is Communism
Is Higher Taxes
Is To Abolish Capitalism

Is Communism
Is Higher Taxes
Is To Abolish Capitalism

Is Communism
Is Higher Taxes
Is To Abolish Capitalism

Is Communism
Is Higher Taxes
Is To Abolish Capitalism

Is Communism
Is Higher Taxes
Is To Abolish Capitalism

Is Communism
Is Higher Taxes
Is To Abolish Capitalism

Is Communism
Is Higher Taxes
Is To Abolish Capitalism

Is Communism
Is Higher Taxes
Is To Abolish Capitalism

Is Communism
Is Higher Taxes
Is To Abolish Capitalism

Is Communism
Is Higher Taxes
Is To Abolish Capitalism

Is Communism
Is Higher Taxes
Is To Abolish Capitalism

Is Communism
Is Higher Taxes
Is To Abolish Capitalism

Is Communism
Is Higher Taxes
Is To Abolish Capitalism

Is Communism
Is Higher Taxes
Is To Abolish Capitalism

Is Communism
Is Higher Taxes
Is To Abolish Capitalism

Is Communism
Is Higher Taxes
Is To Abolish Capitalism

Is Communism
Is Higher Taxes
Is To Abolish Capitalism

Is Communism
Is Higher Taxes
Is To Abolish Capitalism

Is Communism
Is Higher Taxes
Is To Abolish Capitalism

Is Communism
Is Higher Taxes
Is To Abolish Capitalism

Is Communism
Is Higher Taxes
Is To Abolish Capitalism

Is Communism
Is Higher Taxes
Is To Abolish Capitalism

Is Communism
Is Higher Taxes
Is To Abolish Capitalism

Is Communism
Is Higher Taxes
Is To Abolish Capitalism

Is Communism
Is Higher Taxes
Is To Abolish Capitalism

Is Communism
Is Higher Taxes
Is To Abolish Capitalism

Is Communism
Is Higher Taxes
Is To Abolish Capitalism

Is Communism
Is Higher Taxes
Is To Abolish Capitalism

Is Communism
Is Higher Taxes
Is To Abolish Capitalism

Is Communism
Is Higher Taxes
Is To Abolish Capitalism

Is Communism
Is Higher Taxes
Is To Abolish Capitalism

Is Communism
Is Higher Taxes
Is To Abolish Capitalism

Is Communism
Is Higher Taxes
Is To Abolish Capitalism

Is Communism
Is Higher Taxes
Is To Abolish Capitalism

Is Communism
Is Higher Taxes
Is To Abolish Capitalism

Is Communism
Is Higher Taxes
Is To Abolish Capitalism

Is Communism
Is Higher Taxes
Is To Abolish Capitalism

Is Communism
Is Higher Taxes
Is To Abolish Capitalism

Is Communism
Is Higher Taxes
Is To Abolish Capitalism

Is Communism
Is Higher Taxes
Is To Abolish Capitalism

Is Communism
Is Higher Taxes
Is To Abolish Capitalism

Is Communism
Is Higher Taxes
Is To Abolish Capitalism

Is Communism
Is Higher Taxes
Is To Abolish Capitalism

Is Communism
Is Higher Taxes
Is To Abolish Capitalism

Is Communism
Is Higher Taxes
Is To Abolish Capitalism

Is Communism
Is Higher Taxes
Is To Abolish Capitalism

Is Communism
Is Higher Taxes
Is To Abolish Capitalism

Is Communism
Is Higher Taxes
Is To Abolish Capitalism

Is Communism
Is Higher Taxes
Is To Abolish Capitalism

Is Communism
Is Higher Taxes
Is To Abolish Capitalism

Is Communism
Is Higher Taxes
Is To Abolish Capitalism

Is Communism
Is Higher Taxes
Is To Abolish Capitalism

Is Communism
Is Higher Taxes
Is To Abolish Capitalism

Is Communism
Is Higher Taxes
Is To Abolish Capitalism

Is Communism
Is Higher Taxes
Is To Abolish Capitalism

Is Communism
Is Higher Taxes
Is To Abolish Capitalism

Is Communism
Is Higher Taxes
Is To Abolish Capitalism

Is Communism
Is Higher Taxes
Is To Abolish Capitalism

Is Communism
Is Higher Taxes
Is To Abolish Capitalism

Is Communism
Is Higher Taxes
Is To Abolish Capitalism

Is Communism
Is Higher Taxes
Is To Abolish Capitalism

Is Communism
Is Higher Taxes
Is To Abolish Capitalism

Is Communism
Is Higher Taxes
Is To Abolish Capitalism

Is Communism
Is Higher Taxes
Is To Abolish Capitalism

Is Communism
Is Higher Taxes
Is To Abolish Capitalism

Is Communism
Is Higher Taxes
Is To Abolish Capitalism

Is Communism
Is Higher Taxes
Is To Abolish Capitalism

Is Communism
Is Higher Taxes
Is To Abolish Capitalism

Is Communism
Is Higher Taxes
Is To Abolish Capitalism

Is Communism
Is Higher Taxes
Is To Abolish Capitalism

Is Communism
Is Higher Taxes
Is To Abolish Capitalism

Is Communism
Is Higher Taxes
Is To Abolish Capitalism

Is Communism
Is Higher Taxes
Is To Abolish Capitalism

Is Communism
Is Higher Taxes
Is To Abolish Capitalism

Is Communism
Is Higher Taxes
Is To Abolish Capitalism

Is Communism
Is Higher Taxes
Is To Abolish Capitalism

Is Communism
Is Higher Taxes
Is To Abolish Capitalism

Is Communism
Is Higher Taxes
Is To Abolish Capitalism

Is Communism
Is Higher Taxes
Is To Abolish Capitalism

Is Communism
Is Higher Taxes
Is To Abolish Capitalism

Is Communism
Is Higher Taxes
Is To Abolish Capitalism

Is Communism
Is Higher Taxes
Is To Abolish Capitalism

Is Communism
Is Higher Taxes
Is To Abolish Capitalism

Is Communism
Is Higher Taxes
Is To Abolish Capitalism

Is Communism
Is Higher Taxes
Is To Abolish Capitalism

Is Communism
Is Higher Taxes
Is To Abolish Capitalism

Is Communism
Is Higher Taxes
Is To Abolish Capitalism

Is Communism
Is Higher Taxes
Is To Abolish Capitalism

Is Communism
Is Higher Taxes
Is To Abolish Capitalism

Is Communism
Is Higher Taxes
Is To Abolish Capitalism

Is Communism
Is Higher Taxes
Is To Abolish Capitalism

Is Communism
Is Higher Taxes
Is To Abolish Capitalism

Is Communism
Is Higher Taxes
Is To Abolish Capitalism

Is Communism
Is Higher Taxes
Is To Abolish Capitalism

Is Communism
Is Higher Taxes
Is To Abolish Capitalism

Is Communism
Is Higher Taxes
Is To Abolish Capitalism

Is Communism
Is Higher Taxes
Is To Abolish Capitalism

Is Communism
Is Higher Taxes
Is To Abolish Capitalism

Is Communism
Is Higher Taxes
Is To Abolish Capitalism

Is Communism
Is Higher Taxes
Is To Abolish Capitalism

Is Communism
Is Higher Taxes
Is To Abolish Capitalism

Is Communism

Is Higher Taxes

Is To Abolish Capitalism

Is Communism

Is Higher Taxes

Is To Abolish Capitalism

Is Communism

Is Higher Taxes

Is To Abolish Capitalism

Is Communism

Is Higher Taxes

Is To Abolish Capitalism

Is Communism
Is Higher Taxes
Is To Abolish Capitalism

Is Communism
Is Higher Taxes
Is To Abolish Capitalism

Is Communism
Is Higher Taxes
Is To Abolish Capitalism

Is Communism
Is Higher Taxes
Is To Abolish Capitalism

Is Communism
Is Higher Taxes
Is To Abolish Capitalism

Is Communism
Is Higher Taxes
Is To Abolish Capitalism

Is Communism
Is Higher Taxes
Is To Abolish Capitalism

Is Communism
Is Higher Taxes
Is To Abolish Capitalism

Is Communism
Is Higher Taxes
Is To Abolish Capitalism

Is Communism
Is Higher Taxes
Is To Abolish Capitalism

Is Communism
Is Higher Taxes
Is To Abolish Capitalism

Is Communism
Is Higher Taxes
Is To Abolish Capitalism

Is Communism
Is Higher Taxes
Is To Abolish Capitalism

Is Communism
Is Higher Taxes
Is To Abolish Capitalism

Is Communism
Is Higher Taxes
Is To Abolish Capitalism

Is Communism
Is Higher Taxes
Is To Abolish Capitalism

Is Communism
Is Higher Taxes
Is To Abolish Capitalism

Is Communism
Is Higher Taxes
Is To Abolish Capitalism

Is Communism
Is Higher Taxes
Is To Abolish Capitalism

Is Communism
Is Higher Taxes
Is To Abolish Capitalism

Is Communism
Is Higher Taxes
Is To Abolish Capitalism

Is Communism
Is Higher Taxes
Is To Abolish Capitalism

Is Communism
Is Higher Taxes
Is To Abolish Capitalism

Is Communism
Is Higher Taxes
Is To Abolish Capitalism

Is Communism
Is Higher Taxes
Is To Abolish Capitalism

Is Communism
Is Higher Taxes
Is To Abolish Capitalism

Is Communism
Is Higher Taxes
Is To Abolish Capitalism

Is Communism
Is Higher Taxes
Is To Abolish Capitalism

Is Communism
Is Higher Taxes
Is To Abolish Capitalism

Is Communism
Is Higher Taxes
Is To Abolish Capitalism

Is Communism
Is Higher Taxes
Is To Abolish Capitalism

Is Communism
Is Higher Taxes
Is To Abolish Capitalism

Is Communism
Is Higher Taxes
Is To Abolish Capitalism

Is Communism
Is Higher Taxes
Is To Abolish Capitalism

Is Communism
Is Higher Taxes
Is To Abolish Capitalism

Is Communism
Is Higher Taxes
Is To Abolish Capitalism

Is Communism
Is Higher Taxes
Is To Abolish Capitalism

Is Communism
Is Higher Taxes
Is To Abolish Capitalism

Is Communism
Is Higher Taxes
Is To Abolish Capitalism

Is Communism
Is Higher Taxes
Is To Abolish Capitalism

Is Communism
Is Higher Taxes
Is To Abolish Capitalism

Is Communism
Is Higher Taxes
Is To Abolish Capitalism

Is Communism
Is Higher Taxes
Is To Abolish Capitalism

Is Communism
Is Higher Taxes
Is To Abolish Capitalism

Is Communism
Is Higher Taxes
Is To Abolish Capitalism

Is Communism
Is Higher Taxes
Is To Abolish Capitalism

Is Communism
Is Higher Taxes
Is To Abolish Capitalism

Is Communism
Is Higher Taxes
Is To Abolish Capitalism

Is Communism
Is Higher Taxes
Is To Abolish Capitalism

Is Communism
Is Higher Taxes
Is To Abolish Capitalism

Is Communism
Is Higher Taxes
Is To Abolish Capitalism

Is Communism
Is Higher Taxes
Is To Abolish Capitalism

Is Communism
Is Higher Taxes
Is To Abolish Capitalism

Is Communism
Is Higher Taxes
Is To Abolish Capitalism

Is Communism
Is Higher Taxes
Is To Abolish Capitalism

Is Communism
Is Higher Taxes
Is To Abolish Capitalism

Is Communism
Is Higher Taxes
Is To Abolish Capitalism

Is Communism
Is Higher Taxes
Is To Abolish Capitalism

Is Communism
Is Higher Taxes
Is To Abolish Capitalism

Is Communism
Is Higher Taxes
Is To Abolish Capitalism

Is Communism
Is Higher Taxes
Is To Abolish Capitalism

Is Communism
Is Higher Taxes
Is To Abolish Capitalism

Is Communism
Is Higher Taxes
Is To Abolish Capitalism

Is Communism
Is Higher Taxes
Is To Abolish Capitalism

Is Communism
Is Higher Taxes
Is To Abolish Capitalism

Is Communism
Is Higher Taxes
Is To Abolish Capitalism

Is Communism
Is Higher Taxes
Is To Abolish Capitalism

Is Communism
Is Higher Taxes
Is To Abolish Capitalism

Is Communism
Is Higher Taxes
Is To Abolish Capitalism

Is Communism
Is Higher Taxes
Is To Abolish Capitalism

Is Communism
Is Higher Taxes
Is To Abolish Capitalism

Is Communism
Is Higher Taxes
Is To Abolish Capitalism

Is Communism
Is Higher Taxes
Is To Abolish Capitalism

Is Communism
Is Higher Taxes
Is To Abolish Capitalism

Is Communism
Is Higher Taxes
Is To Abolish Capitalism

Is Communism
Is Higher Taxes
Is To Abolish Capitalism

Is Communism
Is Higher Taxes
Is To Abolish Capitalism

Is Communism
Is Higher Taxes
Is To Abolish Capitalism

Is Communism
Is Higher Taxes
Is To Abolish Capitalism

Is Communism
Is Higher Taxes
Is To Abolish Capitalism

Is Communism
Is Higher Taxes
Is To Abolish Capitalism

Is Communism
Is Higher Taxes
Is To Abolish Capitalism

Is Communism
Is Higher Taxes
Is To Abolish Capitalism

Is Communism
Is Higher Taxes
Is To Abolish Capitalism

Is Communism
Is Higher Taxes
Is To Abolish Capitalism

Is Communism
Is Higher Taxes
Is To Abolish Capitalism

Is Communism
Is Higher Taxes
Is To Abolish Capitalism

Is Communism
Is Higher Taxes
Is To Abolish Capitalism

Is Communism
Is Higher Taxes
Is To Abolish Capitalism

Is Communism
Is Higher Taxes
Is To Abolish Capitalism

Is Communism
Is Higher Taxes
Is To Abolish Capitalism

Is Communism
Is Higher Taxes
Is To Abolish Capitalism

Is Communism
Is Higher Taxes
Is To Abolish Capitalism

Is Communism
Is Higher Taxes
Is To Abolish Capitalism

Is Communism
Is Higher Taxes
Is To Abolish Capitalism

Is Communism
Is Higher Taxes
Is To Abolish Capitalism

Is Communism
Is Higher Taxes
Is To Abolish Capitalism

Is Communism
Is Higher Taxes
Is To Abolish Capitalism

Is Communism
Is Higher Taxes
Is To Abolish Capitalism

Is Communism
Is Higher Taxes
Is To Abolish Capitalism

Is Communism
Is Higher Taxes
Is To Abolish Capitalism

Is Communism
Is Higher Taxes
Is To Abolish Capitalism

Is Communism
Is Higher Taxes
Is To Abolish Capitalism

Is Communism
Is Higher Taxes
Is To Abolish Capitalism

Is Communism
Is Higher Taxes
Is To Abolish Capitalism

Is Communism
Is Higher Taxes
Is To Abolish Capitalism

Is Communism
Is Higher Taxes
Is To Abolish Capitalism

Is Communism
Is Higher Taxes
Is To Abolish Capitalism

Is Communism
Is Higher Taxes
Is To Abolish Capitalism

Is Communism
Is Higher Taxes
Is To Abolish Capitalism

Is Communism
Is Higher Taxes
Is To Abolish Capitalism

Is Communism
Is Higher Taxes
Is To Abolish Capitalism

Is Communism
Is Higher Taxes
Is To Abolish Capitalism

Is Communism
Is Higher Taxes
Is To Abolish Capitalism

Is Communism
Is Higher Taxes
Is To Abolish Capitalism

Is Communism
Is Higher Taxes
Is To Abolish Capitalism

Is Communism
Is Higher Taxes
Is To Abolish Capitalism

Is Communism
Is Higher Taxes
Is To Abolish Capitalism

Is Communism
Is Higher Taxes
Is To Abolish Capitalism

Is Communism
Is Higher Taxes
Is To Abolish Capitalism

Is Communism
Is Higher Taxes
Is To Abolish Capitalism

Is Communism
Is Higher Taxes
Is To Abolish Capitalism

Is Communism
Is Higher Taxes
Is To Abolish Capitalism

Is Communism
Is Higher Taxes
Is To Abolish Capitalism

Is Communism
Is Higher Taxes
Is To Abolish Capitalism

Is Communism
Is Higher Taxes
Is To Abolish Capitalism

Is Communism
Is Higher Taxes
Is To Abolish Capitalism

Is Communism
Is Higher Taxes
Is To Abolish Capitalism

Is Communism
Is Higher Taxes
Is To Abolish Capitalism

Is Communism
Is Higher Taxes
Is To Abolish Capitalism

Is Communism
Is Higher Taxes
Is To Abolish Capitalism

Is Communism
Is Higher Taxes
Is To Abolish Capitalism

Is Communism
Is Higher Taxes
Is To Abolish Capitalism

Is Communism
Is Higher Taxes
Is To Abolish Capitalism

Is Communism
Is Higher Taxes
Is To Abolish Capitalism

Is Communism
Is Higher Taxes
Is To Abolish Capitalism

Is Communism
Is Higher Taxes
Is To Abolish Capitalism

Is Communism
Is Higher Taxes
Is To Abolish Capitalism

Is Communism
Is Higher Taxes
Is To Abolish Capitalism

Is Communism
Is Higher Taxes
Is To Abolish Capitalism

Is Communism
Is Higher Taxes
Is To Abolish Capitalism

Is Communism
Is Higher Taxes
Is To Abolish Capitalism

Is Communism
Is Higher Taxes
Is To Abolish Capitalism

Is Communism
Is Higher Taxes
Is To Abolish Capitalism

Is Communism
Is Higher Taxes
Is To Abolish Capitalism

Is Communism
Is Higher Taxes
Is To Abolish Capitalism

Is Communism
Is Higher Taxes
Is To Abolish Capitalism

Is Communism
Is Higher Taxes
Is To Abolish Capitalism

Is Communism
Is Higher Taxes
Is To Abolish Capitalism

Is Communism
Is Higher Taxes
Is To Abolish Capitalism

Is Communism
Is Higher Taxes
Is To Abolish Capitalism

Is Communism
Is Higher Taxes
Is To Abolish Capitalism

Is Communism
Is Higher Taxes
Is To Abolish Capitalism

Is Communism
Is Higher Taxes
Is To Abolish Capitalism

Is Communism
Is Higher Taxes
Is To Abolish Capitalism

Is Communism
Is Higher Taxes
Is To Abolish Capitalism

Is Communism
Is Higher Taxes
Is To Abolish Capitalism

Is Communism
Is Higher Taxes
Is To Abolish Capitalism

Is Communism
Is Higher Taxes
Is To Abolish Capitalism

Is Communism
Is Higher Taxes
Is To Abolish Capitalism

Is Communism
Is Higher Taxes
Is To Abolish Capitalism

Is Communism
Is Higher Taxes
Is To Abolish Capitalism

Is Communism
Is Higher Taxes
Is To Abolish Capitalism

Is Communism
Is Higher Taxes
Is To Abolish Capitalism

Is Communism
Is Higher Taxes
Is To Abolish Capitalism

Is Communism
Is Higher Taxes
Is To Abolish Capitalism

Is Communism
Is Higher Taxes
Is To Abolish Capitalism

Is Communism
Is Higher Taxes
Is To Abolish Capitalism

Is Communism
Is Higher Taxes
Is To Abolish Capitalism

Is Communism
Is Higher Taxes
Is To Abolish Capitalism

Is Communism
Is Higher Taxes
Is To Abolish Capitalism

Is Communism
Is Higher Taxes
Is To Abolish Capitalism

Is Communism
Is Higher Taxes
Is To Abolish Capitalism

Is Communism
Is Higher Taxes
Is To Abolish Capitalism

Is Communism
Is Higher Taxes
Is To Abolish Capitalism

Is Communism
Is Higher Taxes
Is To Abolish Capitalism

Is Communism
Is Higher Taxes
Is To Abolish Capitalism

Is Communism
Is Higher Taxes
Is To Abolish Capitalism

Is Communism
Is Higher Taxes
Is To Abolish Capitalism

Is Communism
Is Higher Taxes
Is To Abolish Capitalism

Is Communism
Is Higher Taxes
Is To Abolish Capitalism

Is Communism
Is Higher Taxes
Is To Abolish Capitalism

Is Communism
Is Higher Taxes
Is To Abolish Capitalism

Is Communism
Is Higher Taxes
Is To Abolish Capitalism

Is Communism
Is Higher Taxes
Is To Abolish Capitalism

Is Communism
Is Higher Taxes
Is To Abolish Capitalism

Is Communism
Is Higher Taxes
Is To Abolish Capitalism

Is Communism
Is Higher Taxes
Is To Abolish Capitalism

Is Communism
Is Higher Taxes
Is To Abolish Capitalism

Is Communism
Is Higher Taxes
Is To Abolish Capitalism

Is Communism
Is Higher Taxes
Is To Abolish Capitalism

Is Communism
Is Higher Taxes
Is To Abolish Capitalism

Is Communism
Is Higher Taxes
Is To Abolish Capitalism

Is Communism
Is Higher Taxes
Is To Abolish Capitalism

Is Communism
Is Higher Taxes
Is To Abolish Capitalism

Is Communism
Is Higher Taxes
Is To Abolish Capitalism

Is Communism
Is Higher Taxes
Is To Abolish Capitalism

Is Communism
Is Higher Taxes
Is To Abolish Capitalism

Is Communism
Is Higher Taxes
Is To Abolish Capitalism

Is Communism
Is Higher Taxes
Is To Abolish Capitalism

Is Communism

Is Higher Taxes

Is To Abolish Capitalism

Is Communism

Is Higher Taxes

Is To Abolish Capitalism

Is Communism

Is Higher Taxes

Is To Abolish Capitalism

Is Communism

Is Higher Taxes

Is To Abolish Capitalism

Is Communism
Is Higher Taxes
Is To Abolish Capitalism

Is Communism
Is Higher Taxes
Is To Abolish Capitalism

Is Communism
Is Higher Taxes
Is To Abolish Capitalism

Is Communism
Is Higher Taxes
Is To Abolish Capitalism

Is Communism
Is Higher Taxes
Is To Abolish Capitalism

Is Communism
Is Higher Taxes
Is To Abolish Capitalism

Is Communism
Is Higher Taxes
Is To Abolish Capitalism

Is Communism
Is Higher Taxes
Is To Abolish Capitalism

Is Communism
Is Higher Taxes
Is To Abolish Capitalism

Is Communism
Is Higher Taxes
Is To Abolish Capitalism

Is Communism
Is Higher Taxes
Is To Abolish Capitalism

Is Communism
Is Higher Taxes
Is To Abolish Capitalism

Is Communism
Is Higher Taxes
Is To Abolish Capitalism

Is Communism
Is Higher Taxes
Is To Abolish Capitalism

Is Communism
Is Higher Taxes
Is To Abolish Capitalism

Is Communism
Is Higher Taxes
Is To Abolish Capitalism

Is Communism
Is Higher Taxes
Is To Abolish Capitalism

Is Communism
Is Higher Taxes
Is To Abolish Capitalism

Is Communism
Is Higher Taxes
Is To Abolish Capitalism

Is Communism
Is Higher Taxes
Is To Abolish Capitalism

Is Communism
Is Higher Taxes
Is To Abolish Capitalism

Is Communism
Is Higher Taxes
Is To Abolish Capitalism

Is Communism
Is Higher Taxes
Is To Abolish Capitalism

Is Communism
Is Higher Taxes
Is To Abolish Capitalism

Is Communism
Is Higher Taxes
Is To Abolish Capitalism

Is Communism
Is Higher Taxes
Is To Abolish Capitalism

Is Communism
Is Higher Taxes
Is To Abolish Capitalism

Is Communism
Is Higher Taxes
Is To Abolish Capitalism

Is Communism
Is Higher Taxes
Is To Abolish Capitalism

Is Communism
Is Higher Taxes
Is To Abolish Capitalism

Is Communism
Is Higher Taxes
Is To Abolish Capitalism

Is Communism
Is Higher Taxes
Is To Abolish Capitalism

Is Communism
Is Higher Taxes
Is To Abolish Capitalism

Is Communism
Is Higher Taxes
Is To Abolish Capitalism

Is Communism
Is Higher Taxes
Is To Abolish Capitalism

Is Communism
Is Higher Taxes
Is To Abolish Capitalism

Is Communism
Is Higher Taxes
Is To Abolish Capitalism

Is Communism
Is Higher Taxes
Is To Abolish Capitalism

Is Communism
Is Higher Taxes
Is To Abolish Capitalism

Is Communism
Is Higher Taxes
Is To Abolish Capitalism

Is Communism
Is Higher Taxes
Is To Abolish Capitalism

Is Communism
Is Higher Taxes
Is To Abolish Capitalism

Is Communism
Is Higher Taxes
Is To Abolish Capitalism

Is Communism
Is Higher Taxes
Is To Abolish Capitalism

Is Communism
Is Higher Taxes
Is To Abolish Capitalism

Is Communism
Is Higher Taxes
Is To Abolish Capitalism

Is Communism
Is Higher Taxes
Is To Abolish Capitalism

Is Communism
Is Higher Taxes
Is To Abolish Capitalism

Is Communism
Is Higher Taxes
Is To Abolish Capitalism

Is Communism
Is Higher Taxes
Is To Abolish Capitalism

Is Communism
Is Higher Taxes
Is To Abolish Capitalism

Is Communism
Is Higher Taxes
Is To Abolish Capitalism

Is Communism
Is Higher Taxes
Is To Abolish Capitalism

Is Communism
Is Higher Taxes
Is To Abolish Capitalism

Is Communism
Is Higher Taxes
Is To Abolish Capitalism

Is Communism
Is Higher Taxes
Is To Abolish Capitalism

Is Communism
Is Higher Taxes
Is To Abolish Capitalism

Is Communism
Is Higher Taxes
Is To Abolish Capitalism

Is Communism
Is Higher Taxes
Is To Abolish Capitalism

Is Communism
Is Higher Taxes
Is To Abolish Capitalism

Is Communism
Is Higher Taxes
Is To Abolish Capitalism

Is Communism
Is Higher Taxes
Is To Abolish Capitalism

Is Communism
Is Higher Taxes
Is To Abolish Capitalism

Is Communism
Is Higher Taxes
Is To Abolish Capitalism

Is Communism
Is Higher Taxes
Is To Abolish Capitalism

Is Communism
Is Higher Taxes
Is To Abolish Capitalism

Is Communism
Is Higher Taxes
Is To Abolish Capitalism

Is Communism
Is Higher Taxes
Is To Abolish Capitalism

Is Communism
Is Higher Taxes
Is To Abolish Capitalism

Is Communism
Is Higher Taxes
Is To Abolish Capitalism

Is Communism
Is Higher Taxes
Is To Abolish Capitalism

Is Communism
Is Higher Taxes
Is To Abolish Capitalism

Is Communism
Is Higher Taxes
Is To Abolish Capitalism

Is Communism
Is Higher Taxes
Is To Abolish Capitalism

Is Communism
Is Higher Taxes
Is To Abolish Capitalism

Is Communism
Is Higher Taxes
Is To Abolish Capitalism

Is Communism
Is Higher Taxes
Is To Abolish Capitalism

Is Communism
Is Higher Taxes
Is To Abolish Capitalism

Is Communism
Is Higher Taxes
Is To Abolish Capitalism

Is Communism
Is Higher Taxes
Is To Abolish Capitalism

Is Communism
Is Higher Taxes
Is To Abolish Capitalism

Is Communism
Is Higher Taxes
Is To Abolish Capitalism

Is Communism
Is Higher Taxes
Is To Abolish Capitalism

Is Communism
Is Higher Taxes
Is To Abolish Capitalism

Is Communism
Is Higher Taxes
Is To Abolish Capitalism

Is Communism
Is Higher Taxes
Is To Abolish Capitalism

Is Communism
Is Higher Taxes
Is To Abolish Capitalism

Is Communism
Is Higher Taxes
Is To Abolish Capitalism

Is Communism
Is Higher Taxes
Is To Abolish Capitalism

Is Communism
Is Higher Taxes
Is To Abolish Capitalism

Is Communism
Is Higher Taxes
Is To Abolish Capitalism

Is Communism
Is Higher Taxes
Is To Abolish Capitalism

Is Communism
Is Higher Taxes
Is To Abolish Capitalism

Is Communism
Is Higher Taxes
Is To Abolish Capitalism

Is Communism
Is Higher Taxes
Is To Abolish Capitalism

Is Communism
Is Higher Taxes
Is To Abolish Capitalism

Is Communism
Is Higher Taxes
Is To Abolish Capitalism

Is Communism
Is Higher Taxes
Is To Abolish Capitalism

Is Communism
Is Higher Taxes
Is To Abolish Capitalism

Is Communism
Is Higher Taxes
Is To Abolish Capitalism

Is Communism
Is Higher Taxes
Is To Abolish Capitalism

Is Communism
Is Higher Taxes
Is To Abolish Capitalism

Is Communism
Is Higher Taxes
Is To Abolish Capitalism

Is Communism
Is Higher Taxes
Is To Abolish Capitalism

Is Communism
Is Higher Taxes
Is To Abolish Capitalism

Is Communism
Is Higher Taxes
Is To Abolish Capitalism

Is Communism
Is Higher Taxes
Is To Abolish Capitalism

Is Communism
Is Higher Taxes
Is To Abolish Capitalism

Is Communism
Is Higher Taxes
Is To Abolish Capitalism

Is Communism
Is Higher Taxes
Is To Abolish Capitalism

Is Communism
Is Higher Taxes
Is To Abolish Capitalism

Is Communism
Is Higher Taxes
Is To Abolish Capitalism

Is Communism
Is Higher Taxes
Is To Abolish Capitalism

Is Communism
Is Higher Taxes
Is To Abolish Capitalism

Is Communism
Is Higher Taxes
Is To Abolish Capitalism

Is Communism
Is Higher Taxes
Is To Abolish Capitalism

Is Communism
Is Higher Taxes
Is To Abolish Capitalism

Is Communism
Is Higher Taxes
Is To Abolish Capitalism

Is Communism
Is Higher Taxes
Is To Abolish Capitalism

Is Communism
Is Higher Taxes
Is To Abolish Capitalism

Is Communism
Is Higher Taxes
Is To Abolish Capitalism

Is Communism
Is Higher Taxes
Is To Abolish Capitalism

Is Communism
Is Higher Taxes
Is To Abolish Capitalism

Is Communism
Is Higher Taxes
Is To Abolish Capitalism

Is Communism
Is Higher Taxes
Is To Abolish Capitalism

Is Communism
Is Higher Taxes
Is To Abolish Capitalism

Is Communism
Is Higher Taxes
Is To Abolish Capitalism

Is Communism
Is Higher Taxes
Is To Abolish Capitalism

Is Communism
Is Higher Taxes
Is To Abolish Capitalism

Is Communism
Is Higher Taxes
Is To Abolish Capitalism

Is Communism
Is Higher Taxes
Is To Abolish Capitalism

Is Communism
Is Higher Taxes
Is To Abolish Capitalism

Is Communism
Is Higher Taxes
Is To Abolish Capitalism

Is Communism
Is Higher Taxes
Is To Abolish Capitalism

Is Communism
Is Higher Taxes
Is To Abolish Capitalism

Is Communism
Is Higher Taxes
Is To Abolish Capitalism

Is Communism
Is Higher Taxes
Is To Abolish Capitalism

Is Communism
Is Higher Taxes
Is To Abolish Capitalism

Is Communism
Is Higher Taxes
Is To Abolish Capitalism

Is Communism
Is Higher Taxes
Is To Abolish Capitalism

Is Communism
Is Higher Taxes
Is To Abolish Capitalism

Is Communism
Is Higher Taxes
Is To Abolish Capitalism

Is Communism
Is Higher Taxes
Is To Abolish Capitalism

Is Communism
Is Higher Taxes
Is To Abolish Capitalism

Is Communism
Is Higher Taxes
Is To Abolish Capitalism

Is Communism
Is Higher Taxes
Is To Abolish Capitalism

Is Communism
Is Higher Taxes
Is To Abolish Capitalism

Is Communism
Is Higher Taxes
Is To Abolish Capitalism

Is Communism
Is Higher Taxes
Is To Abolish Capitalism

Is Communism
Is Higher Taxes
Is To Abolish Capitalism

Is Communism
Is Higher Taxes
Is To Abolish Capitalism

Is Communism
Is Higher Taxes
Is To Abolish Capitalism

Is Communism
Is Higher Taxes
Is To Abolish Capitalism

Is Communism
Is Higher Taxes
Is To Abolish Capitalism

Is Communism
Is Higher Taxes
Is To Abolish Capitalism

Is Communism
Is Higher Taxes
Is To Abolish Capitalism

Is Communism
Is Higher Taxes
Is To Abolish Capitalism

Is Communism
Is Higher Taxes
Is To Abolish Capitalism

Is Communism
Is Higher Taxes
Is To Abolish Capitalism

Is Communism
Is Higher Taxes
Is To Abolish Capitalism

Is Communism
Is Higher Taxes
Is To Abolish Capitalism

Is Communism
Is Higher Taxes
Is To Abolish Capitalism

Is Communism
Is Higher Taxes
Is To Abolish Capitalism

Is Communism
Is Higher Taxes
Is To Abolish Capitalism

Is Communism
Is Higher Taxes
Is To Abolish Capitalism

Is Communism
Is Higher Taxes
Is To Abolish Capitalism

Is Communism
Is Higher Taxes
Is To Abolish Capitalism

Is Communism
Is Higher Taxes
Is To Abolish Capitalism

Is Communism
Is Higher Taxes
Is To Abolish Capitalism

Is Communism
Is Higher Taxes
Is To Abolish Capitalism

Is Communism
Is Higher Taxes
Is To Abolish Capitalism

Is Communism
Is Higher Taxes
Is To Abolish Capitalism

Is Communism
Is Higher Taxes
Is To Abolish Capitalism

Is Communism
Is Higher Taxes
Is To Abolish Capitalism

Is Communism
Is Higher Taxes
Is To Abolish Capitalism

Is Communism
Is Higher Taxes
Is To Abolish Capitalism

Is Communism
Is Higher Taxes
Is To Abolish Capitalism

Is Communism
Is Higher Taxes
Is To Abolish Capitalism

Is Communism
Is Higher Taxes
Is To Abolish Capitalism

Is Communism
Is Higher Taxes
Is To Abolish Capitalism

Is Communism
Is Higher Taxes
Is To Abolish Capitalism

Is Communism
Is Higher Taxes
Is To Abolish Capitalism

Is Communism
Is Higher Taxes
Is To Abolish Capitalism

Is Communism
Is Higher Taxes
Is To Abolish Capitalism

Is Communism
Is Higher Taxes
Is To Abolish Capitalism

Is Communism
Is Higher Taxes
Is To Abolish Capitalism

Is Communism
Is Higher Taxes
Is To Abolish Capitalism

Is Communism
Is Higher Taxes
Is To Abolish Capitalism

Is Communism
Is Higher Taxes
Is To Abolish Capitalism

Is Communism
Is Higher Taxes
Is To Abolish Capitalism

Is Communism
Is Higher Taxes
Is To Abolish Capitalism

Is Communism
Is Higher Taxes
Is To Abolish Capitalism

Is Communism
Is Higher Taxes
Is To Abolish Capitalism

Is Communism
Is Higher Taxes
Is To Abolish Capitalism

Is Communism
Is Higher Taxes
Is To Abolish Capitalism

Is Communism
Is Higher Taxes
Is To Abolish Capitalism

Is Communism
Is Higher Taxes
Is To Abolish Capitalism

Is Communism
Is Higher Taxes
Is To Abolish Capitalism

Is Communism
Is Higher Taxes
Is To Abolish Capitalism

Is Communism
Is Higher Taxes
Is To Abolish Capitalism

Is Communism

Is Higher Taxes

Is To Abolish Capitalism

Is Communism

Is Higher Taxes

Is To Abolish Capitalism

Is Communism

Is Higher Taxes

Is To Abolish Capitalism

Is Communism

Is Higher Taxes

Is To Abolish Capitalism

Is Communism
Is Higher Taxes
Is To Abolish Capitalism

Is Communism
Is Higher Taxes
Is To Abolish Capitalism

Is Communism
Is Higher Taxes
Is To Abolish Capitalism

Is Communism
Is Higher Taxes
Is To Abolish Capitalism

Is Communism

Is Higher Taxes

Is To Abolish Capitalism

Is Communism

Is Higher Taxes

Is To Abolish Capitalism

Is Communism

Is Higher Taxes

Is To Abolish Capitalism

Is Communism

Is Higher Taxes

Is To Abolish Capitalism

Is Communism
Is Higher Taxes
Is To Abolish Capitalism

Is Communism
Is Higher Taxes
Is To Abolish Capitalism

Is Communism
Is Higher Taxes
Is To Abolish Capitalism

Is Communism
Is Higher Taxes
Is To Abolish Capitalism

Is Communism
Is Higher Taxes
Is To Abolish Capitalism

Is Communism
Is Higher Taxes
Is To Abolish Capitalism

Is Communism
Is Higher Taxes
Is To Abolish Capitalism

Is Communism
Is Higher Taxes
Is To Abolish Capitalism

Is Communism
Is Higher Taxes
Is To Abolish Capitalism

Is Communism
Is Higher Taxes
Is To Abolish Capitalism

Is Communism
Is Higher Taxes
Is To Abolish Capitalism

Is Communism
Is Higher Taxes
Is To Abolish Capitalism

Is Communism
Is Higher Taxes
Is To Abolish Capitalism

Is Communism
Is Higher Taxes
Is To Abolish Capitalism

Is Communism
Is Higher Taxes
Is To Abolish Capitalism

Is Communism
Is Higher Taxes
Is To Abolish Capitalism

Is Communism
Is Higher Taxes
Is To Abolish Capitalism

Is Communism
Is Higher Taxes
Is To Abolish Capitalism

Is Communism
Is Higher Taxes
Is To Abolish Capitalism

Is Communism
Is Higher Taxes
Is To Abolish Capitalism

Is Communism
Is Higher Taxes
Is To Abolish Capitalism

Is Communism
Is Higher Taxes
Is To Abolish Capitalism

Is Communism
Is Higher Taxes
Is To Abolish Capitalism

Is Communism
Is Higher Taxes
Is To Abolish Capitalism

Is Communism
Is Higher Taxes
Is To Abolish Capitalism

Is Communism
Is Higher Taxes
Is To Abolish Capitalism

Is Communism
Is Higher Taxes
Is To Abolish Capitalism

Is Communism
Is Higher Taxes
Is To Abolish Capitalism

Is Communism
Is Higher Taxes
Is To Abolish Capitalism

Is Communism
Is Higher Taxes
Is To Abolish Capitalism

Is Communism
Is Higher Taxes
Is To Abolish Capitalism

Is Communism
Is Higher Taxes
Is To Abolish Capitalism

Is Communism
Is Higher Taxes
Is To Abolish Capitalism

Is Communism
Is Higher Taxes
Is To Abolish Capitalism

Is Communism
Is Higher Taxes
Is To Abolish Capitalism

Is Communism
Is Higher Taxes
Is To Abolish Capitalism

Is Communism
Is Higher Taxes
Is To Abolish Capitalism

Is Communism
Is Higher Taxes
Is To Abolish Capitalism

Is Communism
Is Higher Taxes
Is To Abolish Capitalism

Is Communism
Is Higher Taxes
Is To Abolish Capitalism

Is Communism
Is Higher Taxes
Is To Abolish Capitalism

Is Communism
Is Higher Taxes
Is To Abolish Capitalism

Is Communism
Is Higher Taxes
Is To Abolish Capitalism

Is Communism
Is Higher Taxes
Is To Abolish Capitalism

Is Communism
Is Higher Taxes
Is To Abolish Capitalism

Is Communism
Is Higher Taxes
Is To Abolish Capitalism

Is Communism
Is Higher Taxes
Is To Abolish Capitalism

Is Communism
Is Higher Taxes
Is To Abolish Capitalism

Is Communism
Is Higher Taxes
Is To Abolish Capitalism

Is Communism
Is Higher Taxes
Is To Abolish Capitalism

Is Communism
Is Higher Taxes
Is To Abolish Capitalism

Is Communism
Is Higher Taxes
Is To Abolish Capitalism

Is Communism
Is Higher Taxes
Is To Abolish Capitalism

Is Communism
Is Higher Taxes
Is To Abolish Capitalism

Is Communism
Is Higher Taxes
Is To Abolish Capitalism

Is Communism
Is Higher Taxes
Is To Abolish Capitalism

Is Communism

Is Higher Taxes

Is To Abolish Capitalism

Is Communism

Is Higher Taxes

Is To Abolish Capitalism

Is Communism

Is Higher Taxes

Is To Abolish Capitalism

Is Communism

Is Higher Taxes

Is To Abolish Capitalism

Is Communism
Is Higher Taxes
Is To Abolish Capitalism

Is Communism
Is Higher Taxes
Is To Abolish Capitalism

Is Communism
Is Higher Taxes
Is To Abolish Capitalism

Is Communism
Is Higher Taxes
Is To Abolish Capitalism

Is Communism
Is Higher Taxes
Is To Abolish Capitalism

Is Communism
Is Higher Taxes
Is To Abolish Capitalism

Is Communism
Is Higher Taxes
Is To Abolish Capitalism

Is Communism
Is Higher Taxes
Is To Abolish Capitalism

Is Communism
Is Higher Taxes
Is To Abolish Capitalism

Is Communism
Is Higher Taxes
Is To Abolish Capitalism

Is Communism
Is Higher Taxes
Is To Abolish Capitalism

Is Communism
Is Higher Taxes
Is To Abolish Capitalism

Is Communism
Is Higher Taxes
Is To Abolish Capitalism

Is Communism
Is Higher Taxes
Is To Abolish Capitalism

Is Communism
Is Higher Taxes
Is To Abolish Capitalism

Is Communism
Is Higher Taxes
Is To Abolish Capitalism

Is Communism
Is Higher Taxes
Is To Abolish Capitalism

Is Communism
Is Higher Taxes
Is To Abolish Capitalism

Is Communism
Is Higher Taxes
Is To Abolish Capitalism

Is Communism
Is Higher Taxes
Is To Abolish Capitalism

Is Communism
Is Higher Taxes
Is To Abolish Capitalism

Is Communism
Is Higher Taxes
Is To Abolish Capitalism

Is Communism
Is Higher Taxes
Is To Abolish Capitalism

Is Communism
Is Higher Taxes
Is To Abolish Capitalism

Is Communism
Is Higher Taxes
Is To Abolish Capitalism

Is Communism
Is Higher Taxes
Is To Abolish Capitalism

Is Communism
Is Higher Taxes
Is To Abolish Capitalism

Is Communism
Is Higher Taxes
Is To Abolish Capitalism

Is Communism
Is Higher Taxes
Is To Abolish Capitalism

Is Communism
Is Higher Taxes
Is To Abolish Capitalism

Is Communism
Is Higher Taxes
Is To Abolish Capitalism

Is Communism
Is Higher Taxes
Is To Abolish Capitalism

Is Communism
Is Higher Taxes
Is To Abolish Capitalism

Is Communism
Is Higher Taxes
Is To Abolish Capitalism

Is Communism
Is Higher Taxes
Is To Abolish Capitalism

Is Communism
Is Higher Taxes
Is To Abolish Capitalism

Is Communism
Is Higher Taxes
Is To Abolish Capitalism

Is Communism
Is Higher Taxes
Is To Abolish Capitalism

Is Communism
Is Higher Taxes
Is To Abolish Capitalism

Is Communism
Is Higher Taxes
Is To Abolish Capitalism

Is Communism
Is Higher Taxes
Is To Abolish Capitalism

Is Communism
Is Higher Taxes
Is To Abolish Capitalism

Is Communism
Is Higher Taxes
Is To Abolish Capitalism

Is Communism
Is Higher Taxes
Is To Abolish Capitalism

Is Communism
Is Higher Taxes
Is To Abolish Capitalism

Is Communism
Is Higher Taxes
Is To Abolish Capitalism

Is Communism
Is Higher Taxes
Is To Abolish Capitalism

Is Communism
Is Higher Taxes
Is To Abolish Capitalism

9 781720 266082